3

The Return

Other books by Frederick Turner:

Deep-Sea Fish (1968, Unicorn Press)
Birth of a First Son (1969, Christopher's
  Books)
The Water World (1970, Christopher's
  Books)
Shakespeare and The Nature of Time (1971,
  Oxford University Press)
Between Two Lives (1972, Wesleyan
  University Press)
Romeo and Juliet (1974, editor, Hodder &
  Stoughton)
Three Poems from the German (1974,
  Pothanger Press)
A Double Shadow (1978, G.P. Putnam,
  Berkeley)
Counter-Terra (1978, Christopher's
  Books)

The Return

FREDERICK TURNER

Preface by George Steiner

Countryman Press
Woodstock, Vermont

Preface © 1979 by George Steiner

The Return first appeared in the Summer 1979 issue of *The Kenyon Review*.

This edition published October 1981.

Library of Congress Cataloging in Publication Data

Turner, Frederick, 1943-
  The return.

  Poem.
  I. Title.
PS3570.U69R4   811'.54   81-12545
ISBN 0-914378-76-7   AACR2
ISBN 0-914378-75-9 (pbk.)

PREFACE/GEORGE STEINER

A long poem has always been an act of intense trust. The poet manifests his trust in the language, in the reciprocal fidelity of the language to his extensive purpose. A short poem can be a lucky ambush, a surprise collision of high energies as in the fractional instant of a cloud-chamber. A long poem is a companionship, a shared investment, with all the perils of intimacy and of disillusion which such sharing comports. A long poem also bears witness to the poet's trust in the reader. The demands of attention, of acquiescence in style and vision, which a long poem puts to its readers are stringent. To read a long poem is only a technical motion; the first true reading is the first rereading.

The temper of literacy today makes this act of manifold trust even more difficult. The language is loud with the raucous shorthand of political, social, economic fictions. The media charge it with a spurious voltage. We, the readers, are trained to haste, to the expectations of prepackaged reward or shock. The silences, the inward holding of breath, the courtesies of self-forgetting solicited by the long poem, are hard come by. More especially, we have come to dissociate our sense of narrative and of rational discourse, of the everyday pulse of argument, from the means of poetry. We want reality 'straight'.

Thus any long poem written and published today offers and asks for trust. A long poem which enlists the very difficulties, the very obstacles in the way of its own form by seeking to recapture from current prose the powers and responsibilities of adventure, of politics, of the sciences, does more than trust its readers: it honours them.

The Return is a gripping tale of adventure, of broken pontoons and ice-fields, of hunters and fatigue. With the authority of obviousness, Fred Turner reclaims for poetry its antique privilege of heroic action, its right and, perhaps, primal compulsion to tell a story more sharply, with more economy than can that later idiom which is prose. *The Return* has the uncanny spectral concreteness, the high mountain light passing through objects yet giving them a

v

vibrant presentness, which marks Turner's science-fiction. But it is, of course, far more than a concentrated epic of search and of homecoming.

It is a poem about radical politics, the politics at the root of our western condition. It is a critique, none the less poignant for its wryness, of 'the barbarians who don't see themselves as barbarians', of the massacres which inhabit our jaded imaginings. *The Return* is a poem about the leaps of new sensibility, of logic transcended or made playful, which, paradoxically, may be found both in the ancient disciplines of meditation (the Orient in the mind) and in the newest zones of biology and of physics. And *The Return* is, for all its pain, a celebration, an attempt to involve its reader in "the full gaiety of their art of belief" which the narrator experiences in the high cold air and gong-strokes of his venture. Finally, *The Return,* is, in the richest, most traditional sense, a prothalamion, a song sung before and in honour of a nuptial (its points of contact with Spenser are real). It is an account of an education to love. There is no richer schooling.

Wanted: the reader's trust. Reward: a new guest in the house of one's own being and awareness.

GS

The Return

I.

By the banks of the Mekong River there still stands
a ragged geodesic dome built by the crack
shelter group of the Army Corps of Engineers.
Some of its panels are beaten out, some reflect
in jungle bluenesses, shards of bright moonlight.
It blocks the dirt road the Meilinese are building
from the North. Toiling gangs of girls and men
with baskets yoked and carried on the shoulder push
their way past others hard at work with long-shanked spades.

On my right you can see the stalls of the peasantry,
lighted by soft paper lanterns and covered with flowers;
they're selling sweetmeats, hot yams, green meat balls, scented
with ginger and wrapped in big leaves. The whole place
is decked with streamers of crepe paper, purple,
crimson and white, colors of the Revolutionary
People's Democracy of Mei Lin. In Cantonese
the name means 'admirable lotus,' their flag
in many battlefields was found limp with water
wrapped round the skinny body of a dead Lin Rouge
in a ditch at the edge of a paddy-field.

I hear
gongs and many little bells. Everyone stops work.
It's three o'clock in the morning, time to change shifts.
There's an argument whether the dome must come down.
The cadre in charge won't yield to the engineer.
In the end they'll make the road swing to the left
and leave the dome as a park for overnight trucks.
The road, though, must go through to Cholon, there
will be no stopping it. I follow the dispute
in French; the cadre's got a Montagnard dialect
opaque to the captain of engineers. I'm pushed
from behind by a girl in black pajamas; one
of the fresh shift, in from the city on trucks.
She's an oriental Flora from the *Primavera*

1

of Sandro Botticelli.She smiles warmly, apoligises
in beautiful Parisian French. Others stream past,
one girl whom I recognize, lit up in the dim
gold light, a face like a boy's. My Flora runs on.

Sometimes I miss America like a fever:
most, when I'm tempted by an alien beauty.
I can remember the smell of suburban evenings,
the drift of cookout smoke through eucalyptuses,
sound of the washer going into the spin cycle,
the waft of hot suds smelling of jelly beans,
the trip to the market along the manicured
boulevards, the power steering light in mother's
capable hands, the look of duralumin shelves
piled up with produce, blond heads of lettuce,
a thousand peaches, perfect avocados;
color TV at evening, the Dick Van Dyke show,
Father in uniform slips into the VW
for the long weekly commute to Camp Pendleton.

And Father died two weeks ago; I flew back
for two days at the height of my assignment
to watch them shoot the rifles over his body.
Young soldier faces, neat uniforms, white webbing,
jerking chins, caps pulled down over the noses.

Father was a Hawk, and at one time it seemed
important that I should withdraw myself from him;
he believed one had a duty and wearily,
though without complaint, America should bear
the freedom of the world. There was no secret pride
in his belief, I swear it; he thought we'd taken
it over from the British, and naturally
there'd be complaints. Barbarians don't see themselves
as barbarians; they'd defend to the death
their conception of themselves. The British
had their burden from the French, and they theirs from Rome.

He knew a great deal about Greek history,
used to call Europe the Greek colonial empire,
liked to quote Homer's Odyssey. I loved that man,
fought him for years and years.
                              Now in my labyrinth,
the great subcontinent of Indochina,
I've been doing time reporting for United Press
the progress of the war. Here by the ragged dome
I await my new photographer. I recall
five years ago, far over the plains of grass,
the brown shack in the wind where Myers and Diggs
died from multiple injuries sustained by stepping
on a liberated Claymore mine; the choppers
swept over time after time to sheer off at last
from the hard blunt chatter of the Kalashnikovs;
in that hut smelling of gunfire and marijuana
we listened to Procol Harum on Radio Cholon
as the two blacks bled from their arteries. It was
a beautiful day, the sun shone from the blue sky
and the gold grass of the field swished in the wind
of the Cheyennes' rotors.

                              There's a touch on my shoulder.
I turn, surprised, to another brown Oriental face—
Chinese perhaps, but the eyes look straight into mine:
she must be as tall as I am. 'Blanche Yin,' she says.
'They said you'd be here. Tommy couldn't make it,
he's freelancing for *Time*.' Perfectly idiomatic
English, flat incongruous Midwestern accent.
'I'm sorry. You look like a ghost.' She's a large face,
with a mop of springy black hair a la Beatles,
like the faces of certain species of monkeys,
mandrills, or Picasso's *Demoiselles d'Avignon*.
Ironical face. How tall she is! What a deep voice!
(Later I find out she does a marvelous take-off
of Garbo: '*Must* you make an issue of my womanhood?')
Slung on her shoulder, a couple of Pentaxes,

wideangle, telephoto, electronic flash.
She's wearing a watch, and light brown raw silk fatigues—
an affectation here; she's got no figure to
speak of, but like a male ballet-dancer she stands
on one foot and rests the sole of the other,
clasping a thong in her toes, on the side of her knee.
'I came in with the night shift. Couldn't find you, so
they sent me here. I want to start shooting at once.'
I blurt something out, offer her coffee from my flask.

Blanche was born in China, orphaned in 'fifty three.
Her parents had been rich landowning people, shot
by the Maoists. She was spirited out, together
with some Swiss currency, brought up in an orphanage
in Kyoto, Japan. When she was sixteen she came
to America with a Fulbright at Oberlin
studying music and dance. She was there at Kent State
when the students, roaring and bloated with beer
poured down the streets breaking windows; the Mayor in malice
and horror called in the Guard; she was there and saw
when they fell back and knelt in a long ragged line
like the British at Concord, and rattled off their shots;
there's a blurred photo of Blanche in the FBI files
squatted over the corpse of a pottery major
her face drawn with a *Guernica* sorrow; later
she joined for a year the Red Japanese Army
bought guns for the group for the Lod Airport massacre,
was there when the Jews mourned their dead. After that,
as photographs show, her eyes became wider
and she found herself unable to speak, windpipe
paralysed, for five months, in the psychotherapy ward
of the Hospital of the University of Jerusalem.
Since then she's been an observer only, seeing
with eye and with camera all the sorrows
of the world. To the last dark she continues to see.

It turns out Blanche and I were only five feet apart
at the poetry reading they staged in Painted Cave

up in the hills above Santa Barbara;
the morning sun came up over the mountains,
shone on the ancient designs of the sad Chumash,
pale yellow and black and ochre and terra-cotta;
and the poets sat cross-legged in the dust like saints;
we both remembered the harried young man with a beard
and an English accent who kept on worrying
whether or not Gary Snyder would really turn up.
We must have drunk from the same jug of cold Red Mountain
wine wrapped in a paper sack, that went round that morning,
maybe even toked on the same roach. Blue California
dawn, a glitter of webs in the *querca*, dim
haze of jacaranda in the shadowed valley,
smell of eucalyptus, marijuana, love and dust.

Strange how we both miss the same things about America:
not on the face of it the ideas, causes, things
that money can't buy; but not the land itself either;
I get postcards from my sister in Salem, Oregon
with pictures of larch and poplar forests in the spring;
it's very pretty indeed but Blanche and I
are agreed it's not *that* we miss either. What we miss
are the bourgeois trivia of Capitalism:
the smell of a new house, fresh drywall, resin
adhesive, vinyl, new hammered studs; ground coffee
in a friend's apartment in San Francisco, the
first day of the trip; the crisp upholstery
of a new car, its anodized aluminum
dials, the flick of the synchromesh gearshift
white metal gears in their bath of light oil, the glass
tinting the dullest day at the zenith to a
fantastic halcyon glow, the snaking response
of four hundred twenty-eight cubes (yes we know
they wanted the offshore oil); the sound of a fridge
coming on at two in the morning, quiet suburban
night; there was a tenderness, life, a wild hope in all
that technology, there *is* an undeserved good;
the open-channel beam of a powerful stereo
system before the record begins, a subliminal

boom like the sound of a disused cello, dust
in the air drones; we even remember (for now
in the crowded hotel run by a Corsican
whose name is Giuseppe Viola and used
as a barracks—the cadres paid Gus politely
in People's Revolutionary Vouchers—I have seen
perforce in our single room Blanche roll down her
Hong Kong silk stockings, and we are intimate) the smell
of fresh new money, ink smearing slightly, counted out
by the teller of the drive-in bank. It is the things
that money *can* buy we remember, the innocence
of our unfallen materialism when parties
and going on a date were to be unashamedly
looked forward to, when we still swallowed the dear
illusion of value and quality; no,
it was not the ideologically valid
that we with such passion looked back upon; even
the Movement had in it the bouncy high-stepping
joy of the V-W bus, the romance
of revolutionary groceries bought at the A & P,
delicious living underground like Superman,
nobody knowing our real identity, doomed
and shaded by the deadly influence of kryptonite,
wielded by J. Edgar Hoover and the CIA,
the click and the hollow tone of a watched telephone;
that we might have something to hide, that our lives
might be worth the attention of Matt Helm and his
Men from Uncle, in white coats, watching the spools of the
great computer in that mountain in Montana,
monitoring its successive and hysterical displays!
—even the Movement was full of the American Romance.

I wake to see Blanche peering out of the hotel window;
it is a white subtropical dawn, mist steaming off
from the boulevards; the Mekong, flat and bright,
with a lighter, can be seen between rooftops;
I have slept only an hour, it is six a.m.;
Blanche is naked, straight like a child, but for a chaste

6

white pair of panties; purple shadows on a bronze back
where shoulder blades and spine gather the night's dark.
Outside there's activity; there has been gunfire;
one or two cowboys on Hondas have been shot
by mistake, we hear later. Nothing worth reporting.

I can remember being on the crew that covered
the massacre at Long Phuoc. The GIs had left us
with a perfect shooting schedule: first a distant pan
along violet mountains, across bamboos and clouds
for the appreciators in New York and California
of Oriental Art; next, a swift series of vignettes,
the elder with his sparse white beard, flies walking
on his glazed eyes and a leg shredded and splayed;
the mother with the smashed forehead holding a dead child;
the pretty young corpse of a girl, no apparent wound;
the hooches burning still, bright red flames against
the khaki undergrowth; smoke towering in the sky;
and last, the long zoom down the trench where every
attitude of death was composed like a Rodin or a Michelangelo,
one of them naked to the armpits and bleeding.
Enough to feed the great mouth of American fear,
to justify all of our guilt, to make us know
that riches and happiness are bought and paid for
by rape and holocaust. Having known this surely
all our personal failures are as nothing, all our
laziness, weakness, excused by the burden of crime.
They hung over it like flies, those liberals, those
radical American Marxists, in their vicarious
camera-bearing helicopters, shooting the story,
like Babylonian gods sniffing the sacrifice
after the Flood, knowing the sweet shame of propitiation
by the inncocent. And we, in the understatement
of factuality, the exquisite detachment
of the damned, with careful calculation recounted
the whole story. At last America was grown up
enough to make her own horrors. Moral big league;
better, even, than Hiroshima, for the Japanese

were guilty by virtue of their civilization,
they were playing with fire, we wished to be punished
for culture, these peasants at least could be discounted
as innocents. Such was the measure of our self-contempt:
a kind of moral imperialism, whereby we wrought
the world into the image of our guilt and despair.
Cheap stuff, really, figments of a frustrated imagination.

Mocha coffee under plane trees on the boulevard.
The proprietor prepares his own sweet Corsican
croissants; he's going home soon, his trade has shrunk
to a few foreign correspondents. But you can still
get some good hot gossip here. Blanche is in beige,
a model out of *Vogue*. As we are finishing
the man we're expecting appears; he phoned last night.
A snaggletoothed oriental, he tells us he
has contacted Mr. P., they are ready to take us
to see the pots and diggings. We pay him, pack quickly;
take a cyclo to the airstrip. A captured Cherokee
spotter is on the runway. We get aboard,
the craft bounces with a rubber wobble. It spins,
heads out, roars, and lifts. A plain of paddies, green
as emerald. An hour later we're flying
up a terraced valley, between strings of white cloud.
We land by a straggle of villas on a slope.
Midmorning already, it's cool and clear up here.
The pilot, who smiles, chews gum, speaks no English,
pockets up our greasy wad of bills. We're picked up
by a white Mercedes, chauffeur, tinted windows.

Coffee again, this time in a terrace garden
with Colonel Phuong, who is neatly uniformed,
red stripes on his shoulders, unnecessary sunglasses,
smoking a Havana cigar, a luxury
indulged here after the example of Ho Chi Min
by all intellectual cadres of the Mei Lin Rouge
even during the blockade. He walks up and down
before little misty mountains shaped like dog's heads

or sugarloaves, and gestures vigorously.
Now the Americans have gone there's no need
to maintain the supply of heroin that sapped their will;
The inner warlords, swollen with dollars, Swiss francs,
with private armies and expensive weapons systems
bought from the Russians, are now an embarrassment
to the Peoples' Revolutionary Government;
they lack revolutionary discipline. The CIA,
with the same reasons, helps to preserve their concealment.
For obvious political considerations
the PRG cannot afford to expose the Druglords,
so we've been picked to leak the story to the Press
—it's in our interest and also our society's.
Phuong is persuasive, clever, likes his movie role.
Of course the affair will be dangerous: the PRG
will give us assistance but cannot protect us.
Our cover will be a story on the new
archaeological finds of prehistoric pottery;
we will pose as innocent reporters (it's darkest
under the lamp)—amateur archaeologists ourselves
to write up the dig. In the next valley, just over
the border, we'll find, by 'mistake,' the headquarters
of the self-appointed General Nguyen Van Thuoc,
who runs the opium trade. If we survive
we'll get a Pulitzer.

                    What can we say? The deal's made.
And in two days we are bundled, carefully-antiqued
shovels and all, into an unmarked plane and set down
four hours later, on an airstrip in the jungle.
At the horizon there is purple haze,
the unending haze of the Plain of Jars. We're met
by a chap in a jeep, English, in shorts. It's hot.
The camp is a half-dozen tents by a stream.
Wylie, our guide, shows us the prehistoric pots:
we were expecting ugly shards, I think, but
most of these are intact, with delicate shapes

so light they could be set in chaff or straw
and scarcely make it settle. These predate by millennia
the great Greek potters: they are glazed with infinite
negligent sophistication, a pattern of waves,
the colors of ivory, yellow, terra-cotta,
a hint of mad purple and green with diffraction,
one or two tiny burst bubbles on the surface.
Wise craftsmen worked these for an unimaginable
culture when according to previous estimates
man was polishing flints and living in caves.

It is our duty not to implicate our hosts;
they know nothing, we must not arouse suspicion.
Next evening we set out over the hills in a jeep;
below us in the rising mist is a great white house,
fortified, with outbuildings, barracks, parade-squares.
Fields of milkwhite poppies are scattered down the vale,
even this far away we smell the Kingdom of Oz.
We've crossed the invisible border already;
we pass into a lake of new cool air, driving
down to the compound; we are challenged by guards.
Permitted within the outer pentagonal wall
at first all goes smoothly. We explain in Cantonese
that we're with the dig in the opposite valley,
here out of curiosity to pay our respects;
are ushered into the presence of General Thuoc.
With a fine defiance of cliche he is dressed
in a fanciful uniform, night-black leather
and gold; on a sofa beside him reclines
in red silk a person we tacitly christen
the Dragon Lady; we are high, I think, on the
fumes or the fantasy of the place; there are screens
with pink ibises worked in the silk; chandeliers
made of lacquer; Blanche's face twitches, is grave,
concealing amusement. As for me, I'm quite
irresponsible, greet him with antique courtesy.
'Delighted to make your acquaintance, sir.' We're convinced
he is Japanese, left over from the war (later

it turns out our hunch is correct, his real name
is Ugetsu Shigeo, a distant relative
of the great Mitsui armaments family).
How he retains his control of the natives
seems a great mystery; there's no love lost between
the Burmese, Chinese and Thais he commands and their
recent oppressors.

The General rings for a waiter with sake:
it is served to us hot, with a heady brown fragrance;
we tilt the shallow vessels and inquire politely
as to the nature of his enterprise (as if
we did not know) and are of course diverted
by charming generalities. The dragon lady
does not speak. Thuoc is effusive, shows us
prehistoric shards from his own collection.
At length we rise to leave but as we do, at a sign
from our host, we are thrust back into our seats
by a flatfaced guard. It seems we have been betrayed.
Upon inquiry we find it was Snaggletooth
who met us at the cafe; again the cliche
comes true, it's more dreamlike by the moment: traitors
have weaselly faces. There's no point in resisting.
Neither Blanche nor I have any stomach for a
gunbutt in the teeth, the rubber truncheon in the groin,
followed by an inevitable confession.
We tell all, are hustled off, locked in a dark room.

The next days I honestly don't rightly remember.
The first evening they came with a needle and shot us
both up, with high-grade heroin into the inner arm.
The rush was a long lob down a waterfall riding
hysterical pulses of joy down into a pool
where all was incredibly gentle and pale. Still
an edge of infinite shame and pity clung to the mind.
I saw my limbs in the moonlight divided by bars
monstrously elongated like an El Greco
belonging to someone who was if I could recall
to be cared for and comforted, for he was very

11

unlucky. Blanche crawled like a hallucination,
an itch that won't scratch. Sometimes we looked close in each
other's faces, didn't see anyone; sometimes
we paid no mind to the other, in worlds of our own.
The third time they hooked us up, noon of next day,
very hot in the prison, I hallucinated:
not an unusual occurrence with merchandise
as superior as what they were hitting us with.
The whole world retreated and settled in formal lines
like the silvikrin radio waves of Art Deco
or the gaudy classical scenery painted
upon a Kabuki backdrop; there were blossoming
trees with blank animal faces among them
and a bright blue mountain stream pouring down across
center stage, with foam freshly painted. On this stage
took place an odd carnival: to one side a U.S.
Cavalry Colonel with briefcase, tunic well-filled
and snappy brown tie; to the other, stage right,
a vague apparition composed out of muscles
and stress, or the pricklings and smoothness of fever,
needles and pins interspersed with infinite tedious
yardage of burlap and nauseous silk, a thing
I recognized as myself; in between, a shy
Japanese maiden in a kimono stumbling
caught momentarily in a tableau, in some
meaningless flight or surprised greeting, halfway
over the little bridge that you find in willow
pattern over the stream, she has turned her face,
it is that of the girl by the Dome who I once
called Flora.

       But the work is too hard, the pattern
cannot make sense, and presently collapses
into a fugue of shadows and dreams brief as night,
the interminable chatter and flashing away
(reflections darting over a window rapidly
opened and closed)—the eternal idiot calculator
under the skin of the skull.

II.

I cannot tell how many days must have passed there;
there were lucid intervals; Blanche and I reckoned
the General was turning us into slaves to help him
expand his markets and cover his tracks. One morning
we weren't fed or drugged, and we heard shooting;
the guard disappeared, and only came back at nightfall.
He's scared, and we don't understand what he says;
it seems he's going to let us go, but in return
there's something he wants. At last we figure it out:
when we get to America, we'll be his sponsors,
help him obtain an immigrant visa. We agree,
and jumpy already for lack of the drug
we find the jeep where the guard has said it would be;
the place is deserted; in one corner a lazy
billow of smoke darkens and reddens the moon.

When we get to the dig it's empty of people;
the tents are gone, there's only a few heaps of rubbish.
As we search there's the thud of a shot far away;
a spurt of dust is kicked up a few feet from Blanche.
We run for the jeep and drive off into the forest.

So Laos too has fallen. The General must be dead,
murdered probably by his Chinese lieutenant.
With Souvanna Phouma no longer in power
the whole countryside must be alive and up in arms.
We drive carefully back to the compound; still
nobody there. There's firing down at the village.
We load the jeep with jerrycans cold and heavy
with gas that we find in the guardhouse, and food:
there's a soiled map stuck under the sun visor:
we take off quickly into a night of the orient
under a great shoal of stars, the air scented with poppies
and mud, a tinge of cinnamon smoke from the burnt armory.

We're both uncommonly nervous and gay
with a mad hunger for something we know not what.
We're driving north over the starlit dirt roads
of the great Plain of Jars; at times we pass convoys
of trucks going the opposite way. They ignore us.
Southwards there's fighting, we know; we've heard on the radio
several Western reporters were killed in it.
We hope to circle the conflict, cross the Mekong
and come down into Burma.The unease we feel
mounts to an itch and an ache in the bones; at last
our teeth are chattering, though we cover ourselves
with a blanket, and sweat pours down our tired
infinitely tired faces. The addiction has caught.
I can't drive any more, we stop and pull off the road;
Blanche throws up and I cast myself into the grass
and weep.

We are totally lost in this immense
feelingless continent. We wish simply we were home;
for Blanche home itself isn't easy to specify.
And America comes welling up again: the land
of the free and the home of the brave. This time
it's Ohio we miss, qualities too delicate
to be defined; you'll laugh; this is terribly private;
Ohio; the quiet dreariness of it in winter,
fields scattered with snow; the smell of the Ohio
Restaurant at the corner of Maple and Main;
Kresge's at Christmastime; driving on a snowy
evening listening to Handel on Ohio State radio;
getting out of the car, the land flat, the sky blue,
silence, a stand of huge straggly white oaks by the
rest area; the first stars coming out; the moon
lodged in the naked boughs of a big old hackberry tree;
little towns with local politics; *Myers for Mayor*;
Wards having a sale on power tools; the Scioto
half frozen over, this Advent dusk, it all
happening NOW as we lie stranded in Indochina,
now a globe and a half of a day away, down there

under the earth, sleigh-bells on the supermarket muzak!
I'm sorry, you can laugh; my whole body aches;
I want to die and be born again in Ohio.

It's almost morning; I feel myself being propped up,
Blanche has taken my head in her hand, and shaking
is trying to make me drink water from a tin cup.
Her face is deathly pale, her breath smells of sickness,
she cares for me, I'm reminded of the doctor's wife
at the folk festival at Indianapolis:
we went for coffee after the show, she had on
too much makeup, scarcely older than a child,
she sipped timidly, there was Bob Dylan singing
Sad Eyed Lady of the Lowlands on the jukebox;
afterwards we went to a motel; our affair
lasted two months, she had to get an abortion;
she loved me with her thin arms, returned to her
dim sad husband and her allergetic child.
—That was when I was in the city room of a
Midwestern newspaper.

                    We drive northwestwards
most of next day. We choose dirt roads through the hill country.
The peasants stare, we pass their terraces in a cloud
of dust. We plan to talk our way through the roadblock
at Vieng Pou Kha, and cross the Mekong into Burma.
We're both weak and sick, too tired to be responsible;
Blanche though has lost some of the space between her eyes,
I laugh, put my arm around her, we've surely seen the worst.

But the guards are obstinate, tell us to go back;
one of them points his rifle at me while Blanche argues;
they threaten to arrest us if we try to get through.
So we turn and drive north looking for a crossing.
Nothing. An old farmer puts us up for the night.
We're back in opium country, the scent makes us sick.
Next morning Blanche has a long talk with the old man:
the Chinese border is only twenty miles north,

and all of Yunnan province is up in revolt
at the recent death of Deputy Premier Szu.
We have heard nothing of this and inquire urgently:
rightly or wrongly it seems a political murder,
conservative provinces are all up in arms, Mao
on his deathbed cannot restore tranquility.
Chiang Ching, his wife, is suspected of being behind
the assassination.
                    There is a bridge over
the Mekong, says the old man, not many miles north
of the border, in China. No one is watching
the roads, we can get through easily. It's a risk
worth taking. We drive north heading for China.
Neither of us believes any more that we
shall escape. Having found each other what reason
have we to be other or elsewhere than we are?
Nevertheless I write this for you, whether or not
you will never read it.

                    In those bad times you were
very few and far between. Around you the world's
horrible voice hollered from its monster throats.
The whisper, not much more than the hare or the lark
who make their nests in the field, of you who kept faith
could hardly be heard; you lived in the lozenge-shaped
lots ignored by the perplexed builder, with your bamboo
birdcages, your child's elegant letters tacked to
the studio wall, your collection of delicate
heavy expensive brass locomotives (O sweet
Mr. Sparrow, what has become of you, lost
and bereft of a job, puffy from drinking too much!)
with your friend the ex-kamikaze pilot who now
sexes chickens in the Midwest for a living
(a preferred occupation for ex-Kamikaze
pilots, it seems); in your white wooden house among
telephone wires in Wellington, New Zealand;

or among slipcovers in your big frame mansion
in Gambier, Ohio; in your shack in the woods,
in love with a woman who isn't your wife,
unable to write any more; in your awful
apartment in Fort Lee, New Jersey, with your grey-white
Siberian husky as beautiful as Baked Alaska;
in your flat down the road from the Cavendish lab
where you make bronze shiver and soften the crystals;
in your airy-proportioned rooms in Edinburgh
with your twelve children and their wives and their children;
in your old California canyon shaded by *querca*,
dry as a diorama, buzzed by the hummingbirds
golden and green (printing-press out in the garage);
in your hangar in Vancouver where you construct
soft dazzling ships sawn out of aluminum;
in your trout farm where you take off your big rubber boots
and slowly get out your Go board; in Chicago,
South Side, a whole bunch of you, lunatics all;
in Westport, Connecticut, the genius whose name
it took me a year to discover; some students
the kind other students do not like; some old friends
in the city room of the newspaper; and you
in the dull glow of your technology, under
the light of another star—
In those days you were very few and far between:
the sleepy soft one whose nipples hurt when you gave suck
to your baby; the fat one who must be the world's expert
on jujubes and kandy kisses; the absurd
and much beloved homophile who speaks of himself
in the plural, who had an operation
to remove your roll of fat around the waist
(it grew back on your chest, like breasts)—dear Chrysanthemum!
the sharp little exile from a Mennonite family
with your decency, your scholarship, your *saeva
indignatio* and your clever soft Jewess wife;
the artist whose lover has a rare heart condition
so lethal she's the oldest recorded example;

17

the old aunt with your face terribly burned from childhood,
but much-desired; the lesbian lady illustrator,
most sensible of all my friends; that other lesbian
who's so white you're almost albino, can't go out
in the sun; mad Josie, whose husband died at forty
running for a train; the failed priest who wrote a book
on Heidegger; the Jesuit whose cross is the Church;
the physicist turned anthropologist with eyes
so gentle, and your new golden bride in their light;
the blonde Finn who would not show me your latest painting;
the violinist whose book nobody will read
which settles, at last, the question of Virgil's meter;
your wife who found a crystal of snow in your hair
black as the crow, missing your lovely Japan;
the tall art-historian with terrible teeth
and blood-pressure, who connects the Jack-in-the-Box
with the Ark and the Sepulchre; poor dear Paul
you who would sell himself to Public Relations;
the adventurer who wrote to me from Katmandu;
the mad red Swede who plays tennis in the snow;
the Jewish historian who looks like Bozo the Clown;
the lonely Canadian with your cowboy hat;
the anthropologist who invoked the God
Kavula, and who found your own lost father,
a forty years' search, two months after the old man died;
the woman who writes a newspaper for cats;
the woman who taught me to read.

                    None of you
were proletarians, none of you were aristocrats,
You read my poetry for reasons I don't understand.
You heroes with your lovely lives, the glamor of
your gracefulness, were not to know you'd be the pattern
of tomorrow and the true record of our days.

So we pass on into China. As the old man said,
the border is unguarded. There is a bronze light
in the sky; huge hills layered with terraces;

the land is swollen, terminal, it has breathed in
and nothing is uttered in this country. We are
crazier, gayer, sing in the front seat like drunkards,
arms about each other; the pressure's going down,
mountains begin to appear like orange clouds far off.
And as we drive the land changes as if reshaped:
I remember earthquake weather in California.
It's hot, I have my shirt off in the steambath air.
We're in a long valley, then, by and by, we climb
the western ridge and see from the summit the great
swale of the Mekong valley. Still the place is empty,
there are supposed, says Blanche, to be eight hundred million
of us, have they all left for the Moon?

                                             But at the bridge
there's an unexpected surprise: three of the pontoons
have broken away, dangling downstream; the river
is high and brown, making noises all over its face;
in places it's brimmed up to the bank, angry;
small sods of earth are torn off, dissolved as we watch;
and a series of waves make their way downriver.
No way over. So we start up, drive north again,
looking for another place to cross. The air smells
like almonds, there is a great blackness in the north
whose heart we aim at, as if it were a dragon
to be by us destroyed. We pass through a village
and there at last is a person, a little girl simply
pottering about in a most unChinese way.
She pays us little attention, but in the mirror
I see her get up and go inside. We can hear
over the grind of the engine, the little blank shocks
of the thunder, as if we were in a balloon
being patted, or the inside of the ear's being
tampered with. The interior of a vast troubled
organism; the reason there's no people here
is that there is no room for them, they're excluded
by the bestial warm pressure of humanity.

19

We're almost three hundred miles into China
when, as we expected, we're caught. It's a village
beneath cliffs wreathed in mist; suddenly there's a
compound flash in the almost dark, rain white as silver
begins to fall stingingly; a truck full of soldiers
drives out of a side street in front of us; Blanche
greets the commanding officer with 'comrade' in
Cantonese; but nothing avails, we are taken
to the local commune headquarters building,
treated courteously, fed, while the lady commissar
in grey uniform, with high official voice
telephones the authorities. Blanche and I
feel like two naughty boys side by side on a bench
tittering, scared. My eye wanders over the walls:
a picture of Mao, Lenin looking exactly
like a campus radical professor, very fierce;
a calendar. I don't understand the Chinese,
but the date reads twenty-five. It's Christmas Day. I
begin to whistle 'tis the season to be jolly;
Blanche, becoming aware, collapses helplessly
in oriental gurgles. Outside, the Polar airmass
is fighting with the Tropics: Yang against Yin,
a dark curl enclosing a white flash of lightning
with at at its heart a black spot, a cataract of dazzle.
The rain drums on the tin roof. We eat hot rice
washed down with lettuce soup, very good I have to say.
They lock us up singly against vigorous protest.
They are puritans and have established early
the fact we are not married. They have what the Germans
call *tierische Ernst,* bestial seriousness.
We remain there for several days in cells
pleasant enough, converted hastily we find
from seminar rooms where cadres expounded Mao's Thoughts.
It's cold outside. The windows mist up at times,
but the life of the Commune can be seen going on
without any obvious sign of disturbance.
We consider it wise not to mention the death
of Comrade Deputy Premier Szu. The place

works like cloned insects, colonial ants or bees,
the most fundamental social organisation.
At times we get sessions on Revolutionary
Consciousness. We're grateful to them for their trouble,
but wish they'd leave us together more. For Blanche and I
have fallen in love; I think of her constantly;
all the ancient cliches are true, there is love
hidden in every fold of her mouth and cheek,
in the sweet hang of her silken clothes, in the hint
of bosom under the square brown buttons of her blouse;
in the tilts and the shrillnesses of her deep voice,
in the shaded reserve of her eyes, her clever wit,
her brown humanness, the moles on forearm and neck,
the way she keeps her beautiful black tresses clean.
When we meet we're like teenage sweethearts, I open
doors for her, and set her chair carefully, she laughs
at me and lets her hand linger by mine. Our skins
have become magical receptors, our breaths
mingle along the cold meeting halls, our captors
don't know how to deal with us, we're setting a dreadful
example. The old toothless lady who sweeps up
has taken to giving us villainous grins
and the ideological cadre halts in her
speech, when we sighing exchange fervent glances;
we are eroticizing the entire commune.

From hints and guesses we gather that we are the eye
of a local political storm. Nobody knows
whether our capture can be construed as a plus
or a minus. The Yunnan Commissar whose name
is Yuen, wants to take credit but dare not;
here in the village the local authorities
are politically linked with the Party machine
in Szechwan, which leans to the faction of Chiang Ching.
At last orders come in from K'un Ming, the capital
of Yunnan province. The cadre is gloomy. Blanche
learns from the cleaning lady we are to be shot.
It is the simplest solution, at least deprives

21

leftist factions of leverage in the struggle.
Our hosts, however, refuse to capitulate;
we gather we are to be taken to Szechwan
and the lack of compliance blandly explained
as an oversight. There in Szechwan, in the railhead
at Ch'eng-tu, we'll be back in Peking's control.
We're pleased, needless to say, but cannot, however,
take the whole situation as seriously
as it deserves. As if in a game we are moved
from checker to checker; we've lost the distinction
between the black and the white; have become for the time
aware only of borderlines.

                    We are bundled
into the jeep, wearing Communist serge greatcoats.
It is cold, with gusts of rain; the plastic sidewindows
mist up, but we see on our right the blue-grey sheet
of a lake. The village where we were caught is called
Hsia-Kuan; we're being taken the long way around,
through country controlled by our friends, north to Chamdo,
then west through the dark ranges of Shaluli Shan.
The slopes are pouring with spates, the crests are hidden
in cloud, each hill has a hat, a mist-mantle huge,
the chill metal freezes our hands, there's no heater.
And now we enter that strange region where the three
rivers, the Yangtse, the Mekong and the Salween
burst from the Himalayan chains in the valleys of gloom
ten miles apart, to water the various Edens
and Hells of Siam, Indochina, Cathay.
It's hard to breathe. We're at the throat of the world.
Blanche and I huddle together, happy only
in each other. Helpless we've been passed up the long
birth-canal of the Indochinese subcontinent
into its deep groin; and presently it starts to snow.

In Te-ch'in the authorities have been alerted;
we are caught in a rest-house only ten miles
from Tibet. We're afraid we'll be shot; but Yunnan

has changed his mind, recognizes the *fait accompli*,
has sent men to escort us. Thus, if our capture
is good, *they* will take the political credit;
if ill, they can blame it all on the plots of Szechwan.
It looks as if our 'friends' have been circumvented;
but Chung Nin, the driver, is able unobserved
to phone from the hot inn kitchen his allies
in Chamdo. We're met at the border by a truck
full of lean Tibetan faces, soldiers heavily
armed with automatic weapons; the men of Yunnan,
the tables turned, are sent back again, dark with rage,
and an older officer jumps into the seat
by our driver, orders him to go on, to follow
the truck, and they fall into deep conversation.
The truck turns off the main road left toward the river;
with an angry shrug, our driver does the same.
Blanche's face is aflame with attention; I find
from her later that the Tibetan authorities
have decided that we are a nuisance, are going
to let us escape into Burma and blame it
on their political enemies in Szechwan
and Yunnan. The truck bucks and wallows down the slope
and there below us is the great river, shrunk now
and altered in name, but still to us the Mekong
that has denied our passage for so long. It seems
there may be a way out of Asia, a light at
the end of the tunnel. Ahead is a stone bridge,

which we cross. It is New Year's Eve. We are taken
over a pass between cliffs and down a ravine
where we cross the Salween, and up again like a dream;
we find ourselves in an empty valley deep in snow.
At the head of the valley is an enormous cloud.
The air is very thin. We stop, get out. Silence.
They push us roughly at the jeep, point up the road
marked with black stones, toward the border of Siam.
The Thala Pass. Late sun strikes under the wrack.
The snow is lit with orange. Before us to the west

is the immense shadow of the mountain-wall, blue
as the mystical lights along the runways of airports.
We are almost hysterical, running a fever
in this dry cold, our lips chapped and our eyes ache
with the chill. We climb into the seats and drive
for America, tires bumping and crushing the snow.

III.

At the head of the pass we see the sun in its
last green flash. We gasp in the thin air. To the north
and west are a thousand mountains banked up like clouds
on a summer's day over cornfields but the corn
here is coarse blond snow. At the border the guards
on the Chinese side ignore us. There's nobody
on the Burmese side. Darkness falls. The jeep stumbles
down the hill. The air warms, thickens, takes on the smell
of laurels. We reach Gawai at midnight. The year
is nineteen seventy-six. Two hundred years ago
the revolution of the thirteen colonies began.
There is no hotel, we find the police station.
No one speaks each other's language, we're bedded down
for the night in a cell. It is still cold. We share
a thin bunk, we shiver uncontrollably;
Blanche is long and naked like a peeled branch; my flesh
has known nothing so warm and so gentle, it seems,
and has roughened; I fear for her satiny skin.
As lovers now we are joined at the root in a
great rush or blow like the recoil of a rifle:
in Coition, the prime symbol of America.
At this root the nuclear family is nourished;
it is this revolutionary simplicity
on which the nation is founded. America
is here and now in this long passage where it comes
that I am most male, most adult in my risktaking;
where she is the most female in her carefulness;
where we exchange the value of our juices;

24

where the Tao splits into subject and object;
where we lose, and gain, and lose the distinction of sexes;
where Blanche exploits me and I yield to her mastery;
where I exploit her and she submits to mine;
where each creates a desire in the other, a desire
to be satisfied only by the gift of the self,
giving each irresistible power over the other.
In this we both have the vote, we pass from primary
to election. Her mouth is open and her eyes,
I find, are open and wet with tears. Neither of us
has any form of contraception; we will humbly
go forward into life like any married couple,
hand in hand through the fire and the ocean, to be
the factory of love and value for the world.
On us all things will depend: there is only this
after all, let us look at the world realistically:
nothing else is worth so much, it's mankind's greatest discovery.

Later that night we are woken inexplicably.
Then we feel it again, a wobble of the whole world,
a few unpredictable jolts, and a silence.
Earthquake. Then we hear in the distance a sharp crack,
like silk giving suddenly when it is ripped,
and a boom that builds and continues as if in
the barrel of some immense musical instrument,
a thudding and rolling and bumbling, a few sighs,
and silence again. Now shouting begins. We're drowsy
and don't care too much; we turn on our sides like spoons
and doze off.
    In the morning we're taken down
the what we take to be City Hall. The village
straggles along a muddy street, it is misty;
a torrent crashes past in a gorge that is choked
with dim rhododendrons; enormous slopes bulge up
on either side in the fog, the light's flat and white,
the bright blue quilts of the brown women washed out and pale.
We meet the mayor, who's like a Burmese version

of Edward G. Robinson, toadlike, crapulous,
clever, with rings on his finger, and now we find
that he too's a communist; hearing our story
of escape out of China, he's inclined to send us
straight back to his masters; doesn't believe we were freed
and let go; it's in vain we point out it would be
an embarrassment to those he wishes to please
if we were made to return; but, ironic, he says
that we have no credentials, how does he know
that we aren't political refugees?
We demand that he telephone south to his chiefs;
he refuses. It seems we are to go back.

We're in luck though. The earthquake last night set off
a series of avalanches into the pass;
it's blocked and may take several days to be cleared.
We're pushed into an outer room while Edward G.
consults with his peers. Blanche and I are exhausted
at last; now when we seem to be closest to home
our endless wanderings start all over again.
In the room there's a couple of women with babies,
a monk in a saffron robe and shaved skull, a young man
wearing a passable suit, with a briefcase. Blanche
and I hash over our plight. After a moment
we're suddenly aware that the monk is paying
the keenest possible attention to our talk
and we in turn look more carefully at him.
We notice his color and bone structure are not
like the others; in fact, he's white. We break off.
'Excuse me,' he says, apologetically,
in the style of a US college professor,
'I could not help overhearing your conversation.
Allow me to introduce myself.' He is shy
and formal, but in his cheeks there's a trace of a flush,
the odd hysteria of one who's been under therapy.
'My name was Phaedrus Pierce, I'm an American.
Now I am named Chandragupta after one of
the masters. I live in the big monastery

up at the head of the valley in Tazungdam.
Can I help?' We both at once recognize the name.
'Can you by any chance be *the* Phaedrus Pierce?
The writer of *Lotos and Crescent Wrench*?' He nods.
'But everyone said that you'd flipped, they'd put you away
in a looney bin somewhere.' Blanche interrupts:
'I heard from a friend who runs a bicycle shop
in Annapolis that someone walked in and asked
for a collapsible bicycle you could fold up
and stow in a boat. He signed his name on the check
P.H. Pierce. Was that you?' He grins. It turns out
he spread the rumor of his incarceration
and then disappeared; he had a friend in Vancouver,
British Columbia, who built in a disused hangar
outside the airport, huge white ships sawn and welded
out of aluminum—and here I break in,
knowing mad Frank just as well as he does. Small world.
Anyway he bought from Frank a fifty-foot junk
after an ancient design, had it shipped all the way
over the continent, launched it into the Chesapeake,
sailed it alone, helped by a tiny computer
whose heart is a newly-invented inertial
guidance device with a nuclear gyroscope
according to patents developed by Fraser,
the founder of the International Society
for the Study of Time. Down the east coast he sailed,
crossed the Caribbean, barely avoiding
hurricane Sophy, threaded the isthmus of Panama;
he burst into the Pacific in his silver ship,
felt the great quiet that comes when the wind is astern;
he was caught in the Humboldt, the God of the Sun
painted upon his sail. The leading edge of the spars
of his vessel carried compacted the ghosts
of Balboa and Cortez; he hunted the sun
westward over the datelines; he saw a sperm whale
breach, and a million miniature eels played round his keel
in the translucent doldrums rayed like a halo
with spokes round his head's shadow in the beams of the moon;

and he smelt, sailing across the transverse salmon-pink
waves of the orient dawn, down the slope of the world,
the spice and spikenard smell of the island of Java.

So he tied up at anchor in Bangkok and like
Thurber's little admiral on the wheel he rode
his folding cycle through the jungles of Siam
till he reached the eerie thresholds of Tibet.
He shaved his head and spun the wheel; he's here to clinch
the sale of certain monastery lands, being still
more worldly than his anchoritic templemates.

So we tell our new friend of our predicament.
Back in prison two nights later the barred window
is sawed out with a fine carbide-tipped keyhole saw;
we are led a mile by a hooded figure, packed
into a battered Mercedes-Benz; at early dawn
we reach the village of Tazungdam and begin
the slow climb to the great ramshackle stone building
that staggers up the ridge. Below it is a chasm;
it has a thousand windows; parts of it have been
disused for over a century; others are new;
others yet, built in the time of William Shakespeare,
have recently been restored. The sky is clearing;
it is dark navy blue with a whisper of cirrus;
a fresh wind blows from the snowfields, the close little
glacier that debouches on a small milky pond.
A few stunted pines in the hollows. Tufts of grass.
We get out of the car. Everything's silent and final.

We find the long uneven corridors crowded;
they're preparing a festival. These monks belong
to an heretical Ch'an sect; Tazungdam lies
at the junction of Northern and Southern Lamaism;
to the West there are Hindus and Jains, to the East,
nearby, Communists and followers of the Way.
Over seven centuries their calendar, based
on the precession of the perihelia

of the planet Mercury, has got out of phase
with that of the Chinese; the New Year's Festival
is to be held on the fifteenth of January,
not, as with the feast of Tet, on the thirty-first.
Like their time, their dogma has undergone
strange transformation. There's an odd Tantric strain
in their asceticism; we will find out later
in the dim gold and candleglitter of their ritual
the full gaiety of their art of belief.
We are shocked and bound by an enormous sublim-
inal hum. It is the striking of the bronze.
We're taken to a clean cell over a torrent,
seated by monks who bring in razors and bowls;
they shave off Blanche's beautiful black hair and in
the lovely garnish of a boy she watches me
as I undergo the same transformation.
We are clothed in saffron. I feel absurdly
the tingle of election, the throb of initiation
in my bowel and spine; Blanche, as we are led forth
catches me hard by the hand; they have not trimmed
her beautiful fingernails.

                Nor have we yet seen
Mr. Pierce, Chandragupta as he's now called.
It is important that he not be involved;
as an alien he might be deported. Only now,
disguised against any pursuit, may we join him.
He takes us to pay our respects to the Abbot,
the Atisha Lama, named Padmasambhava.
He is seated in a great vault lit with candles,
his throne carved with snakes and swastikas; he has on
a long red robe well fitted at his narrow waist;
his chest is broad, his full mouth fringed with wispy beard.
His voice is the voice of the Wizard Sarastro
in Mozart's *The Magic Flute*—as deep as a bear's.
He speaks, we find, excellent English; took a First
in Greats—Trinity College, Oxford. He greets us
not formally, but with natural courtesy;

does not allude, despite our expressions of gratitude,
to the risks he is running; takes us up to the window;
in the sun the flash of snow on the Thala Pass
whence we came, can be seen. It seems, says the Lama,
that the earliest Men came over these passes
two and a half million years ago; if Man
evolved anywhere, the fossil evidence points
to the valleys of Indochina. 'So Mei Lin,'
Blanche says ironically, 'was the original
Eden?' 'It would appear so,' murmurs the Abbot.
What have we done? The past is no refuge.

As we leave the chamber we see the great Lama
lean over to speak with the priest Chandragupta;
he puts his hand on the shoulder of the younger man;
their faces are very close; in the candlelight
it is so beautiful I shiver once, and feel
an answering tremor in Blanche's long hand.

In the next days we're trained in the way of meditation.
It's decided we'll be sent over the Diphuk Pass
into India, but the deep snow forbids it
for the present. We're introduced by our teacher,
an old monk with frayed gloves that show a gnarled knuckle,
to the high wisdom of the Brihad-Aranyaka:
how the source of all actions is the body
for by the body all actions are performed;
but even as the body is behind all action,
so Brahman is behind the body;
how the source of all forms is the eye,
for by the eye all forms are seen;
but even as the eye is behind all forms
so Brahman is behind the eye;
how the source of all names is the word
for by the word all names are spoken
but even as the word is behind all names
so Brahman is beyond the word.
And now as a caterpillar, reaching the end

of a grassblade, gropes across to another and draws
itself over; or as a traveller, reaching
the head of the pass, crosses from one valley to
another, whose river flows to a different sea;
so I pass over to another state of existence.
I see Blanche rarely, with her shaven head; I am
gently constrained to consider the mandala;
its concentric squares and circles are felt as a map
of the soul; the whole subcontinent seems like a maze
at whose center I discover myself, my Atman;
I pass through circles and circles, each of them
carrying souls who cry out to me; and at last
(I am, I am told, a good student) I find the Peace
whose faces are those of the Body, the Eye, and the Word.
Now through my flesh, fed purely on rice, there comes
a high chill, a rest that sinks to the base of the spine
with a shudder that loosens the bands of the neck
and makes itself felt in the throat as a chant,
a mantra whose name is the jewel in the heart
of the lotus. My diaphragm flutters, though I
know it not; my eyes are blind, and I feel in my skull
the unuttered light, the pure phos-phoros
of the inner eye of Time.
                           But now Up becomes Down,
I have reached the earth's core, the weight of the world
is reversed, I climb through the spirals, aware
of myself once more, aware of my awareness;
led now by my master Chandragupta I climb
up the mountain, encounter once more my Blanche
who's got thinner and pale; the mandala's turned
inside out, and becomes a sign of evolution
as each successive level is passed: atemporal,
prototemporal, eotemporal, chemotemporal,
biotemporal, nootemporal: cortex
mushrooms around the seething, transforming midbrain:
even as a probability fluid, floating
in phase-space, or a photonic soup

bloats and fingers out in its first seconds to a
full-scale universe; even as the mind knows
to hear itself speak; even as the brain-stem
blossoms in the fetal baby, so I turn back
and climb toward tension, the knowledge of death;
I'm in love again, and now in the draughty galleries
of the great Lamasery we sneak times to meet.
The last days have seemed like a single breath taken
and held and breathed out; the snows are beginning to melt
in the mountains, the whole place prepares for the feast
of the morrow, the day of New Year. It is to be
the Year of the Dragon: Wealth and Good Health,
Long Life and Good Luck. We help the young monks
put up the decorations, prepare the great stage
in the inner court of the place, for the play
and the dancing. It will be our festival too,
as Americans: our Fourth of July.

On the morning of the fifteenth we must fast.
The place is hushed. In the evening the celebrations
will begin.
             First there is a pageant
of the eighteen deities, the red and black demons,
the snake devil, and the fiery Tiger God. The monks
are seated in the courtyard. Next comes in a priest
in a coat of mail with ornaments of flags,
a high hat with tufts of wool, and flags, and effigies
of human skulls. He burns in a blue brazier
small images of men and animals, yak-hair
and knots of wool. Now the play begins, to the scream
of many flutes, the click of wooden blocks, the bang
of gongs; two figures, winged, approach each other, fight
with spurs attached at wrist and ankle: the spirits
of Lang Dharma the emperor who would destroy
the Lamas, and his enemy Lō Pön the great saint
of the Tantrik-Yogacharya School, representing
anagogically the forces of the Yin and Yang.
There is a cosmic battle, Lō Pön is slain,

rises again with the sun of the new year
riding on a dragon. The monks have got very drunk.
There follows a procession of the Gods:
the Buddhas, Sakya, and the celestial buddhas,
the Dhyanibuddhas, Bodisats (Maitreya,
Manjusri, Vajrapani, Avalokita,
Tara, Marici), tutelaries such as
Vajrabhairava, defenders of the faith,
Dharmapalas, and the demon-lords, the Dakkinis,
the eight orders of lesser divinities,
the eight orders of country-gods, personal gods,
saints, Tantric wizard-gods whose chief is Padmasambhava,
played by our friend Chandragupta.

A billion candles burn and incense billows; bells
tinkle in the blue gloom, a feast of delicacies
is borne in, with candied peacocks, great gingered carp,
whole lambs shellacked with gold and rice wine; steaming
mounds of sweetmeats, allowed to go a little beyond
the edge of fermentation; gallons of rice- and
millet-wine borne in in Chinese jars and poured into
the flat black dishes of the priests; firecrackers burst
and a young monk is burned on the hand; all the windows
of the great house, seen from across the valley, must be
aglow with the riot of the celebration.

IV.

But in the morning we must set out over
the Diphuk Pass, for India. The track's impassable
to wheeled vehicles still, but word has come through
that the authorities have wind of where we are:
there's no time to be lost. So in the cold dawn we
(slightly hungover) prepare the parkas and packs
the monks have kindly provided. As we tighten
the straps, a young monk slips in; he is pale, warns us
that Edward G. and his goons, in a jeep, right now
are being stalled off at the gates. We're hurried down

33

ancient staircases and ramps and let out by a
postern into the snow. We have maps but no guide
for even one absence will surely be noted.
The police chief has a list of the Tazungdam priests.

Following the map we trudge up the slope. We must cross
a ridge and in the next valley pick up the trail
of the Pass. As we walk in the dim sunshine veiled
by a high film of cloud, our spirits rise again
though over the last weeks of hope and reversal
we've become wary, observers no longer
but actors, with all the circumspection of actors.
Blanche is leaner, the man in her seems predominant;
her slight pout has given way to a grin of effort;
when we gain the further valley we find the hut
of a yak-herding family; the family head
is a big-bosomed flatfaced intelligent woman
whose five small husbands (in loincloths only, even
at this great altitude), like children, respond
petulantly, but at once, to her orders.
We laugh at that.

            All day we walk steadily
up the long valley. The thin air catches in chest
and windpipe, and ears are dumb in the great silence.
The small wind which blows about the valleys and hills
on pleasanter days, parches our skin. We're remote,
pure act in a pure world of being. We become,
like heroes, a trifle flip about these hills, spend
the night in a rest-house where we drink rice wine
and sit at a yak dung fire under low rafters
scratching for fleas. That night, fuddled with altitude,
I dream and dream. We are up in the pass. It's cold.
The snow is deep. I hear a talking in my head.
We lie down in the snow. We're choked. But it seems
I must, desperately, get up and urinate.
I struggle up into the numb wind and prepare
to relieve myself. But at once the fluid is frozen,

I am rooted, absurd, so to say, to the spot.
So Blanche must cut me free. Circumcised thus, the snow
ceases to fall; and at once it's a thousand years
back in the past, we've discovered the North-West passage;
the dream speeds up, I catch images of old friends,
briefly Father.

In the morning we get over
the border without any trouble. There's even
a pleasantly courteous border-guard in a hut,
somewhat bored by his job, not upset in the least
by our absence of any identification.
He phones us a taxi from Kahao which turns out
to be a battered Studebaker whose driver
is blessedly ready to trust us for the fare.
It's all too easy. We still feel hunted and must try
to open our shoulders, breathe easy as one might
where a hostile world did not always surround us.

There remains little to tell. We are taken, after
some days, to Gauhati on the Brahmaputra,
put up at the house of the local commissioner:
a big mansion with peeled stucco hallways, tapestries
blown out by a soft warm wind, smelling of turmeric,
plaster-lime, *ghi*, and the fertile dust; the courtyard,
dense with the early jasmine, becomes the place
where we walk each day; we telephone the Calcutta
bureau-chief, it seems there will be two weeks' delay.
By the river we count the species of trees:
Pandanus many-rooted, and Banyans, the Bodhi
being one: *Ficus religiosa,* whose fruit
conduces to visions; Palms, the fiery Betel,
the Areca, *Phoenix silvestris* of the sweet sap;
many lush spready Plantains; the Plane or Platan,
the Zinnar-tree whose palmate leaves brush heaven;
and in the low hills over the farmland we find
Azaleas, Myrtles, masses of Rhododendron,
leafy Bamboos, sweet wild Tea, triumphant Laurel.

One time I remember, we were sitting under
a jolly pink picture of Ganesha, the elephant god
of Good Fortune; through the branched window we saw
the sacred blue river, the green and purple hills;
three handsbreadths above them the fantastic vision
of a snowcapped range of mountains, lesser outriders
of the Himalayas, where two great crystal plates
meet, as they do no other place on the globe,
and the subcontinent of India, in its
millenial drift from the broken world-island
of Gondwanaland, threw up by its impact
into Asia that colossal barrier, we see
in the river a long sandbank, and beyond it
moving steadily, a dhow with a white lateen sail,
a brown sailor at the tiller, leaning outboard
to scan the dim waters, hung from his neck a string
of spotted cowrie-shells and bright blue coloured glass.
We hear in the next room the murmur of Eepie
the memsahib, and her sisters-in-law.

                                   Our papers,
passports, and money, arrive in February.
We take the train to Calcutta and fly west to
Tehran, Athens, Rome, London, New York. Stunned, sleepless,
we are debriefed in a neat white soundproofed room,
acoustic ceilings, blue upholstered presidential
rocking chairs, a woodgrain formica desk with a
duralumin ashtray (made from the nacelle of a
crashed and recovered U-2, with the Eagle crest)
by a gentleman from the CIA. He has on
a blue Bones blazer, white shirt, blue tie, grey slacks,
a Florida tan. We're amused by the charade,
stagger out having done our bit for the Republic
into the cannibalistic embrace of the Press.
We're beginning to get angry with our country
in a new way. Later we're taken out to lunch
by a publisher's agent who's somehow both timid
and arrogant, talks of the 'breadth' of 'our concerns,'

'what publishing's all about,' 'material' that
will 'move,' 'placement on the market,' 'authorial
priorities,' 'writing to sell'; he wants us to 'do
a book for him' that will 'hit the realities
of the Far East.' We get angrier and angrier;
Blanche is pale about the lips, the man is odious—
his aftershave, his Bill Blass suit, his confidential
whine, his bonhomie—they send us out fighting for air
from the panelling of the Algonquin into
the dear old streets of dying New York. There's something
vile about his sexuality, it's servile,
hothouse, insistent. A fourteen-year old punk
makes an amateurish attempt to mug us, I
slap him round the ears and send him away. They're all,
the Yalie spy, the tele-journalists, the man
in the Algonquin and the pale yellow beggar
from Bedford-Stuyvesant, all of them looking
for value to suck off, for a source of judgement,
a sacred river of truth they can foul with their mouths;
like the smart alec in old movies who hitches
a free ride on a plank carried, oblivious,
by two other men, they want to get theirs without
giving; they're all into consumer research,
the Gallup Poll, finding out what other people think,
and trying to sell them, packaged in plastic,
their own excrements; or, like our wretched brigand,
worshipfully eating up the shit of others
—poor sheep's breath!

       In the paper we read of the trial
of Patricia Hearst, the most famous person in
the world; in the evening I rage through New York, Blanche
tries to placate me; get drunk; break the nose of a
poor harmless creep who tries, because of my half-shaved
head, to pick me up in a bar. Where is their pride?
as a friend of mine with fine eyes used to ask
of people at T-groups; I wish for a moment
I were buried again in China or had stayed

with poor Phaedrus in Tazungdam. But in that too
I realize I'm not alone; each damned soul here
has a hideaway too, whether it be an
authentically-weathered converted barn in Weston,
Connecticut, or at the infinite bosom
of old Mamma Smack whose milk we saw ooze from
the poppies of Thailand ten thousand miles away.
Nothing I feel has any originality.
In the *New York Times Book Review* on Sunday, I
see it all written down in execrable English.
We get a plane to Columbus, Ohio. We have
to start again.

       So. First we must found a 'we'
whose voice we can speak in: it's whoever will join.
Next we pronounce the Universe Good. (We rent
a house in a town called Liberty, begin digging
a garden.) We consider the world alive, asking
questions, feeling out in long laciniate runnels
of incompressible probability fluid
or abulge like the lobes of the walnut or the
cerebral cortex, the only viable way
in its own terms, as fast as it can, drawn out
at the speed of light which is also the speed of
knowledge, by the suction of future, or nothing.
From this the stars, the stones, the plants, the animals,
each eating with holy relish the corpse of its
forebears. Again, we pronounce it good. (Spring comes;
the woodland is laced with the nuptial dogwoods;
we decide to get married.) Next we examine
the birth of the cultures of Man, their arts and their
languages; brushing aside the wars and the pogroms,
the beating of children, the death camps, the murders,
the slaves—this is all par for the course, the only
course that we have—and again we bless it and so
make it holy. (I start a small advertising firm:
I am good at my job, only accept decent
business; my copy is written in fair English,

and properly spelt. Blanche begins a second degree
in Greek and Cultural Anthropology.)
We consider our class, which is the bourgeoisie:
most guilty, most humble, most gifted of classes,
having given Humanity all of its art
and its thought; we speak Good of it, name it, and so
it is so. Here, almost, we falter, cannot keep
a straight face; but this tremor is fear and betrayal
and cannot be countenanced: we sit through the rictus
until it subsides, repeat the blessing and now
the burden's departed. (Blanche misses two periods—
pregnant the night of New Year, the first birthday
of America, red white and blue!) At last we look
at our friends, our acquaintance, ourselves. There is
a maker of harpsichords, a builder called Blaine,
a farmer called Briggs and my artist who's now
finished the picture she would not show me: it's here
before me, a rainbow that joins Earth with Heaven.
No halo of moral justification
surrounds them, but still they're all undeniably
Good. Ourselves—Why, if we were not blessed, we should
not be able to bless. I forgive, for my part
even the publisher, even the spy. The arg-
ument's circular. (This summer we plan to start
a new magazine. All it will print will be stories
of Praise.)
               Not that we live in great solemnity.
We're happy, are not much concerned for permanence.
Those who, disposed to find us odd or dull, leave us
alone, find us well pleased to be ignored. Those who
are skeptics of our happiness—let them be
happier than we and then surely in their content
they could not grudge our joining in their happiness.

Blanche in her blossomy calico
leans to turn on the radio:
a Coffee Cantata by Johann Bach.

Morning coffee in the kitchen, where
the sunlight strikes
through the blue air
upon white clapboard, window glass. The glare
is dazzling, lights up the green spikes
of indoor plants: impatiens, pink
begonias, and phloxes by the sink.

Upon the kitchen table a brown hand
(a cigarette,
a golden band)
blazes with brown light, naked, and behind
a grapefruit halved and pink is set
beside the steamy coffeepot:
the one warmed by the sun, the other hot.

It's Fischer-Dieskau on the radio
with a hoarse flute,
continuo
on harpsichord, a coarse brown bass below.
Amber strings repeat and mute
the striding tenor. These things are
the glory of the bourgeois-secular.

Each moment the next moment generates.
Unflaggingly
earth celebrates.
The senses, uncompleted, seek new states:
the potent coffee-chemistry,
the music, and the leaves unfurled.
Quotidian dawn of the sunlit world!